Published by Creative Education
123 South Broad Street, Mankato, Minnesota 56001
Creative Education is an imprint of The Creative Company

Designed by Stephanie Blumenthal
Production Design by Patricia Bickner Linder

Photographs by: FPG International, GeoIMAGERY, Grace Davies Photography,
International Stock, Laure Communication, Peter Arnold, Inc., Smithsonian
Institution, Team Husar, and Tom Stack & Associates

Library of Congress Cataloging-in-Publication Data

Richardson, Adele, 1966–
Gems / by Adele Richardson
p. cm. — (Let's Investigate)
Includes glossary.
Summary: Examines the origins and study of gemstones,
including facts about mining and jewelry making.
ISBN 0-88682-993-3
1. Precious stones—Juvenile literature.   [1. Precious stones.]
I. Title.   II. Series: Let's Investigate (Mankato, Minn.)
QE392.2.R53   1999
553.8—dc21   97-43738

4 6 8 9 7 5 3

GEMS

ADELE RICHARDSON

Creative Education

GEM

Most gems form in places about 100 miles (161 km) below the earth's surface.

GEM

*The largest pearl ever found weighed 454 **carats** and measured two inches (5 cm) in length.*

Right, turquoise and gold pendant; far right, malachite beads

All through history people in every part of the world have worn some kind of jewelry, either for decoration, or because they believed it had "magic" powers. Often this jewelry has been made out of the colorful, shiny stones we call gemstones.

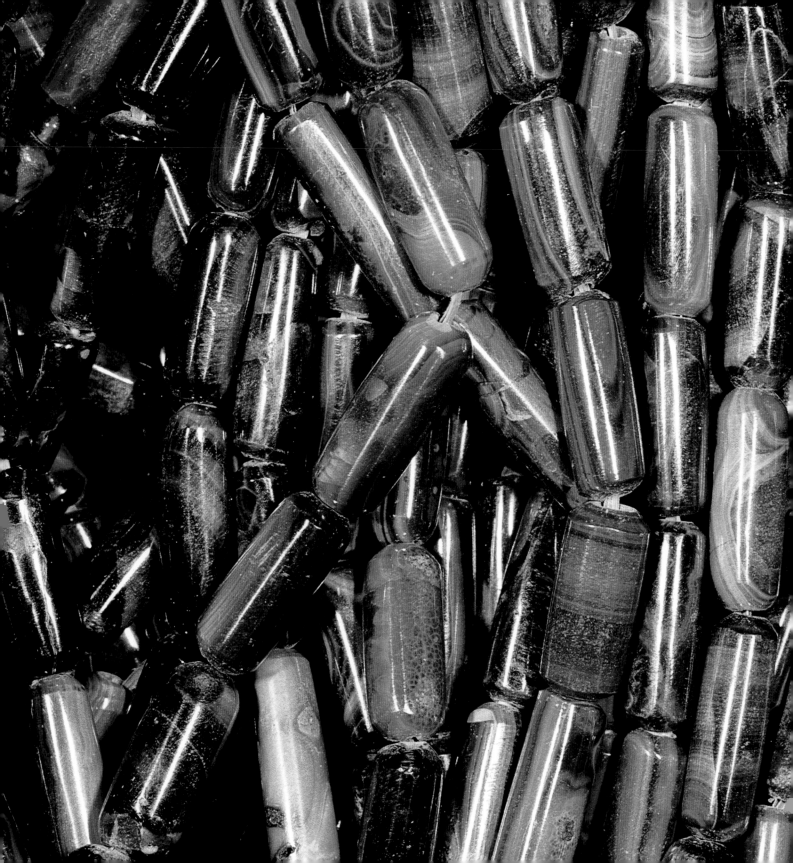

GEM
CROWNING

Royalty and rulers have had impressive gems set into their crowns and weapons all through history.

Above, Russian crown jewels; right, raw opal

GEM FORMS

Almost all gemstones are formed below the earth's surface. Some are brought to the surface by **mining.** Others are brought up through natural processes, such as the eruption of a volcano. Sections, or plates, of earth can move deep below the earth's crust to reveal gemstones. Even underground streams can push them up to the surface.

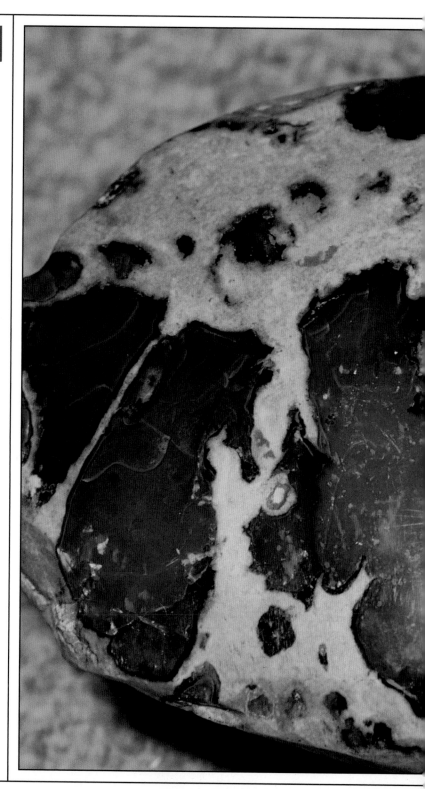

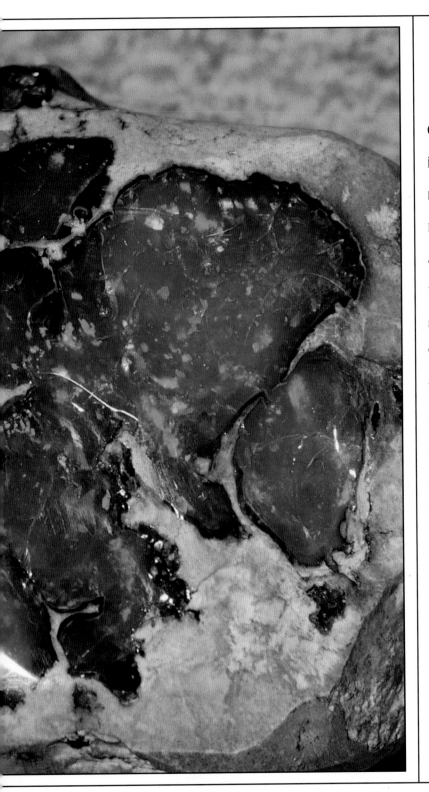

Real gemstones are formed in three ways. One method is the cooling and crystallizing of molten, or hot, melted rock. They can form from a solution, like salt crystals that are left after sea water **evaporates.** They are also formed when rocks or stones change after being exposed to high pressure, heat, and moisture. These types are called metamorphic gems. Some examples of metamorphic gems are jade and garnet.

GEM
COLOR

Most diamonds look colorless, but the few that are colored are especially valuable and expensive to buy.

Below, cut, polished diamonds

GEM

A saltwater oyster dies when a pearl is removed from it.

GEM

IMPERSONATOR

Though pearls are prized for jewelry they are not actually considered real gemstones.

Above, oyster and pearl; right, pearl necklace

Gemstones are **minerals,** meaning they are found naturally in the earth. There are also four types of gems that are made by plants and animals. These four gems are pearls, coral, amber, and **jet.**

A pearl is interesting because it starts out as a foreign object, such as a grain of sand, that gets inside an oyster's shell. This is very uncomfortable for the animal and it will protect itself by coating the object with layer after layer of **nacre.** The round formation of nacre eventually becomes a pearl.

9

GEM
RUSSIAN

The rarest garnet is green and is found only in Russia's Ural Mountains.

Above, Russian "chromium" garnet

GEM

TRAPS

Amber is actually sap that once seeped out of prehistoric trees and hardened. Usually it's clear enough to see through, but bugs and leaves may have been trapped inside.

GEM

BONES

Coral is actually the skeletal remains of little sea animals.

Right, the Logan sapphire necklace; far right, giant topaz

GEM QUALITY

Stones must have certain qualities to be considered gems. Most importantly, they must have beauty. The stones must also be hard and tough enough to resist a lot of wear, and they must be rare enough for people to value them. The beauty of a gemstone depends on one or more of four things: its color, its brilliancy, its "fire," or a special visible feature, if it has one.

GEM
WINKING

When a gemstone with a "cat's-eye-effect" is turned, it looks like an eye opening and closing.

Above, aquamarine in stages: rough, cut, and polished; right, rough diamonds—one weighs 90 carats

Gemstones can be found in almost any color. The garnet, which is best known as a deep red, is found in nearly all colors except blue. The sapphire is most recognized for its blue color, but this stone can also be found in many other colors. It can be white, yellow, green, violet, and even black. The diamond looks colorless, but most of these stones have a tiny bit of coloring. If there is a lot of color in a diamond, it becomes extremely valuable and is called a "fancy." The blue and pink diamonds are the most valuable; red diamonds are very rare.

I f a diamond is clear and clean it is called a "diamond of the first water." A stone's brilliancy measures how shiny it is or how much it reflects light. Brilliancy depends on how clear the stone is and if it was cut and polished properly. Brilliancy never depends on the color of the gem.

The "fire" of a stone is a rainbow effect. When a diamond is turned in sunlight it flashes piercing colors in all directions. These flashes of color are the "fire." Only transparent stones that have brilliancy can flash fire.

Some gems, like the tourmaline, have the ability to change color when viewed from different angles.

Left: diamonds and jeweler's tools

GEM

FACT

Diamonds and other gems have been found in the bottom of streams.

There are a few stones in the quartz and beryl families that have a special visible feature called a "cat's-eye-effect." This effect is a reflection from inside the stone that resembles an eye looking at you. Some stones may actually have more than one cat's-eye-effect appearing in them. If this happens, the stone is said to have an **asterism** quality. Some varieties of quartz and garnet have this quality.

Right, Rosser Reeves star ruby; far right, black opal

Another stone with a special visible feature is the opal. It even earned its name from the reflection it has: **opalescence.**

Each gemstone has its own qualities of **hardness** and **toughness.** Hardness is the stone's ability to keep from getting scratched or worn down. Toughness describes its ability to keep from breaking.

GEM

TRUE-BLUE

The Hope Diamond is the largest known blue diamond at 45.5 carats. It can be seen today at the Smithsonian Institute in Washington, D.C.

GEM

EXPENSIVE

Large rubies, being very rare, are many times more valuable than diamonds of the same size.

Right, opal mining in Australia; far right, the Hope diamond

DIAMOND MINING

Mining for gemstones can be as simple as digging a tunnel, or it can be a complicated method that involves heavy machinery, explosives, and **hydropower.** Diamond mines are located on all continents. The diamonds are usually found in long, narrow rock masses that go straight down into the ground. These masses are called pipes. The pipes contain a rock called **blueground.** When miners see this rock, they know there is a good chance of finding diamonds.

GEM
SHOCKING

When amber is rubbed it charges with static electricity. The Greeks called it elektron.

Quartz herkimer, or "false" diamond

Many diamonds are found at or near the earth's surface in **dikes.** A dike is a wall that forms after molten rock bubbles up through the earth. The rock cools near the surface and becomes solid.

In 1962, diamonds were taken from the ocean floor for the first time. To do this, miners use a rubber hose 12 inches (30 cm) wide and extend it from a barge to the ocean floor. The hose sucks up gravel and sediment like a huge vacuum cleaner. Miners average one diamond for every ton (2,000 pounds or 450 kg) of gravel removed from the ocean floor. This is actually better than mining blueground, which averages one diamond for every 20 tons (40,000 pounds or 18,000 kg) mined.

No two pearls are ever exactly the same, and pearls that are perfectly round are rare and very valuable.

Left, Venetia diamond mine in Africa; below, raw aragonite

GEM

Diamond-tipped instruments are used to drill into the earth for rock samples.

Right, a gold and aquamarine pendant with pearls; far right, facet-cut gemstones

CUTTING AND POLISHING

O nce gems are taken from the earth they must be cut and polished before being made into jewelry. Since the beauty of a gemstone will depend on the way it is cut, a poor cut will lower the value of a stone. If cut properly, brilliant reflections should appear across the whole stone, causing its value to rise.

Cutters will use a spinning wheel of sandstone or grindstone to gently make the cuts into the gem. This is called **facet cutting.** It is used only with transparent stones.

Another method is the **cabochon cut.** In this process the stone isn't cut to bring out brilliant reflections. Instead, the stone is smoothed and rounded. The gems used for this type of cut are round and have a polished curved surface and a flat bottom. Long ago, all gems were cut this way. Then facet cutting was discovered and was shown to produce much more beautiful gems. Now, only stones with the cat's-eye-effect are cut with the cabochon cut.

21

GEM

Gems are weighed in metric carats. One carat equals one-fifth of a gram. That's 200 milligrams or 0.007 ounces.

GEM
HARDNESS

Diamonds are the hardest known gem. Jewel cutters use instruments with diamond tips to cut other diamonds.

Right, a diamond cutter from Denmark; far right, raw, uncut opal

To polish gems, cutters press the stones against a canvas-covered wheel that has been soaked in special chemicals. They may use their fingers to hold the gem, or they may cement the stone to a small iron rod. As the wheel spins, it gently buffs the gem until it is shiny and smooth.

GEM
POETRY

The Chinese consider jade to be the most valuable gemstone. They even carve poems about Chinese emperors into priceless jade bowls.

Above, uncut opals; right, jewelry made from jet stones

SUBSTITUTE GEMS

Today, people can make substitutes for gemstones. The substitutes are often cheaper to make and just as beautiful as real gemstones. There are two types of gem substitutes: synthetics and imitations.

Most synthetic gemstones are made from a mixture of powdered chemicals, such as pure aluminum, that are fed slowly into an extremely hot flame. Once the mixture cools, it hardens and can be cut and polished to look like a real gemstone.

An imitation gem looks like a natural gemstone, but it is not formed the same way. Often a cheaper, more easily found **inorganic** material that has a glassy or crystal appearance is used. Once it is cut and polished, it too looks like a real stone. If a synthetic or an imitation is made correctly, only an expert can tell the difference between the substitute and a real gem.

Amber has been discovered in chunks weighing as much as 18 pounds (8 kg).

Above, raw stribnite

GEM
AMERICAN

Only a few diamonds have been found in the United States— in Pike County, Arkansas, and in the Upper Peninsula of Michigan.

GEM
GLASS

A rhinestone is a type of substitute gemstone made from a special kind of glass called strass.

Right, raw amethyst; far right, polished malachite

GEM SUPERSTITIONS

Over the years, **superstitions** have developed about some gems. As late as the 1700s, people used gems ground down into powder to "cure" or "prevent" diseases. Opals were once thought to bring good luck, and then later they were thought to bring bad luck. A purple gem called amethyst was once thought to cure headaches and toothaches. The blue sapphire was once used as protection against evil.

GEM

SUPERSTITION

The diamond was at one time thought to cure nightmares.

GEM

F A C T

The tunnel of the Kimberley mine in South Africa is over 3,500 feet (1,000 m) deep. That's over half a mile (.80 km)!

Eventually, science proved that these "cures" don't work. That didn't stop people from believing though. Even today there are superstitious people who will insist that gems have special "magical" abilities.

The science of gems is called gemology. Along with jewelry making, gemology is a popular hobby for people of all ages in all parts of the world. Some people choose jewelry making for a career.

GEM

AUSTRALIAN

The rarest and best quality black opals are found only in Australia.

Left, facet-cut gems; above, cabochon-cut black opals

GEM

Rock crystal is a type of gem. If it's found in big enough pieces it can be carved into plates and vases.

GEM
ROYAL

The largest diamond ever found, the Cullinan, weighed in at over 3,106 carats (one and one-third pounds, or .6 kg). Some of the smaller stones cut from it are in the Royal Scepter and State Crown in England.

30

Top right, gem geodes; below right, turquoise; far right, raw ruby

There are books available in most public libraries on how to make jewelry. Gem materials, equipment, and classes can also be found in most large cities. Gemstones have been around since the earth was formed. They are used in science as well as for art and beauty. They come in so many different types, sizes, and colors that nearly everyone can afford to own a gem of some kind. While some are very rare, some are plentiful. All gems are an important resource that add beauty and sparkle to the world we live in.

Glossary

Asterism is the term used to describes a stone with more than one cat's-eye-effect.

A blue-grayish rock that is very hard and may contain diamonds is called **blueground.**

Cabochon cut (CAB-uh-shun) is a method of cutting a gemstone until it is smooth and rounded.

The weight of gems is measured in metric **carats.** One carat equals one-fifth of a gram.

Dikes are long, thin masses of rock that look like walls.

When water **evaporates,** the sun's heat turns the water into vapor, or gas.

Facet cutting is a method of cutting a gemstone with a spinning grindstone or sandstone.

Geodes are round stones with hollow centers that are lined with crystals or minerals.

A stone's ability to keep from getting scratched or worn down its **hardness.**

Hydropower is electric power that is produced by water. Forms of matter that are found naturally in the earth but are not from plants or animals are **inorganic.**

Jet is a type of fossil wood related to brown coal.

Minerals are forms of matter found naturally in the earth; the were not made by plants or animals.

Mining means to dig or burrow into the ground in search of valuable materials.

The smooth coating produced by oysters that protects the animal inside its shell is called **nacre** (NAY-ker).

The pearly reflection from inside gemstones such as opals is called **opalescence.**

Superstitions are false ideas that some people believe.

A stone's ability to keep from breaking is its **toughness.**